THE GOSPEL GOES TO WORK

GOD'S BIG CANVAS OF CALLING AND RENEWAL

Stephen R. Graves

Adapted for groups by
KRIS DOLBERRY

LifeWay Press®
Nashville, Tennessee

Published by LifeWay Press® • © 2017 Stephen R. Graves

No part of this book may be reproduced or transmitted in any form or by any means, electronic or mechanical, including photocopying and recording, or by any information storage or retrieval system, except as may be expressly permitted in writing by the publisher. Requests for permission should be addressed in writing to LifeWay Press®; One LifeWay Plaza; Nashville, TN 37234-0152.

ISBN 978-1-4627-4279-0 • Item 005793395

Dewey decimal classification: 248.84
Subject headings: WORK \ CHRISTIAN LIFE \ FAITH

Unless indicated otherwise, Scripture quotations are taken from the Christian Standard Bible®, Copyright © 2017 by Holman Bible Publishers. Used by permission. Christian Standard Bible® and CSB® are federally registered trademarks of Holman Bible Publishers.

To order additional copies of this resource, write to LifeWay Resources Customer Service; One LifeWay Plaza; Nashville, TN 37234-0113; fax 615-251-5933; phone toll free 800-458-2772; order online at lifeway.com; email orderentry@lifeway.com; or visit the LifeWay Christian Store serving you.

Printed in the United States of America

Groups Ministry Publishing • LifeWay Resources • One LifeWay Plaza • Nashville, TN 37234-0152

CONTENTS

About the Author   4
How to Use This Study   5
Tips for Leading a Small Group 6
Introduction   8

WEEK 1
The Gospel and Work
10

WEEK 2
Individual Baseline
24

WEEK 3
Individual Blue Sky
38

WEEK 4
Organizational Baseline
52

WEEK 5
Organizational Blue Sky
66

WEEK 6
Take the Gospel to Work
80

ABOUT THE AUTHOR

Stephen R. Graves is a strategist, an executive coach, and an author. At any given time he's working with a handful of remarkable executives leading large global organizations and young social entrepreneurs who are just starting out. Steve has authored more than a dozen books that teach people how to flourish in their life and work. He holds an MDiv from Southwestern Baptist Theological Seminary and a DMin from Dallas Theological Seminary.

When Steve isn't consulting or writing on strategy, leadership, or impact, you can find him backcasting in the cold, clear rivers of northwest Arkansas. To explore Steve's content and read his weekly blog, visit stephenrgraves.com.

HOW TO USE THIS STUDY

This Bible study provides a guided process individuals and small groups can follow to explore the need to take the gospel to work and ways they can do so. This study is divided into six key topics:

1. The Gospel and Work
2. Individual Baseline
3. Individual Blue Sky
4. Organizational Baseline
5. Organizational Blue Sky
6. Take the Gospel to Work

One week of Bible study is devoted to each of these topics, and each week is divided into five days of personal study to be completed between group sessions. In the personal study you'll find biblical application and interactive questions that will help you understand and apply the teaching and coaching about how to take the gospel to work.

In addition to the personal study, six group sessions are provided to spark gospel conversations. Free downloadable videos are also available to supplement the group sessions. These videos feature discussions between author Steve Graves and people who are taking the gospel to work. Some of the video participants reflect on key ideas in several individual interviews, and a promotional video is also available. All of these videos can be downloaded at no cost from LifeWay.com/GospelGoestoWork.

Each group session is divided into three sections:

1. "Connect" focuses participants on the group session's topic of study.
2. "Explore" guides the group to engage with the main ideas of the group session and with a relevant Scripture passage.
3. "Transform" guides the group to respond to and apply the group session's teaching.

If you want to go deeper in your study, you may want to read the book on which this Bible study is based. *The Gospel Goes to Work* (KJK Inc. Publishing) is ISBN 978-1-9407-9414-3.

TIPS FOR LEADING A SMALL GROUP

Prayerfully Prepare

Whether you are facilitating this study for the first time or are inspired to guide another group through it as a result, prepare for each group session with prayer. Ask the Holy Spirit to work through you and the group discussion as you point to Jesus each week through God's Word.

REVIEW the weekly material and group questions ahead of time.

PRAY for each person in the group.

Minimize Distractions

Do everything in your ability to help people focus on what's most important: connecting with God, with the Bible, and with one another.

CREATE A COMFORTABLE ENVIRONMENT. If group members are uncomfortable, they'll be distracted and therefore not engaged in the group experience.

TAKE INTO CONSIDERATION seating, temperature, lighting, refreshments, surrounding noise, and general cleanliness.

At best, thoughtfulness and hospitality show guests and group members they're welcome and valued in whatever environment you choose to gather. At worst, people may never notice your effort, but they're also not distracted.

Include Others

Your goal is to foster a community in which people are welcome just as they are but encouraged to grow spiritually. Always be aware of opportunities to include and invite.

INCLUDE anyone who visits the group.

INVITE new people to join your group.

Encourage Discussion

A good small-group experience has the following characteristics.

EVERYONE PARTICIPATES. Encourage everyone to ask questions, share responses, or read aloud.

NO ONE DOMINATES—NOT EVEN THE LEADER. Be sure your time speaking as a leader takes up less than half your time together as a group. Politely guide discussion if anyone dominates.

NOBODY IS RUSHED THROUGH QUESTIONS. Don't feel that a moment of silence is a bad thing. People often need time to think about their responses to questions they've just heard or to gain courage to share what God is stirring in their hearts.

INPUT IS AFFIRMED AND FOLLOWED UP. Make sure you point out something true or helpful in a response. Don't just move on. Build community with follow-up questions, asking how other people have experienced similar things or how a truth has shaped their understanding of God and the Scripture you're studying. People are less likely to speak up if they fear that you don't actually want to hear their answers or that you're looking for only a certain answer.

GOD AND HIS WORD ARE CENTRAL. Opinions and experiences can be helpful, but God has given us the truth. Trust Scripture to be the authority and God's Spirit to work in people's lives. You can't change anyone, but God can. Continually point people to the Word and to active steps of faith.

Keep Connecting

Think of ways to connect with group members during the week. Participation during the group session is always improved when members spend time connecting with one another outside the group sessions. The more people are comfortable with and involved in one another's lives, the more they'll look forward to being together. When people move beyond being friendly to truly being friends who form a community, they come to each session eager to engage instead of merely attending.

ENCOURAGE GROUP MEMBERS with thoughts, commitments, or questions from the session by connecting through emails, texts, and social media.

BUILD DEEPER FRIENDSHIPS by planning or spontaneously inviting group members to join you outside your regularly scheduled group time for meals; fun activities; and projects around your home, church, or community.

INTRODUCTION

Four Categories

Every Christian on the planet falls into one of four categories in regard to taking the gospel to work:

- Those who don't think the gospel has any relevance or place in everyday work life
- Those who think the gospel belongs at work but only in the realm of private attitudes
- Those who want to take the gospel to work but find themselves confused, unmotivated, or alone in that aim
- Those who've discovered that the reach, power, and intent of the gospel can revolutionize any worker's approach to any work in any setting

Authenticity

I remember having a breakfast meeting with a CEO in Chicago who said, "It's being involved in the rigor of the business world day in and day out that keeps my life of faith strong." After pondering his comment, I think I understood what he meant. The pressure, demands, and choices endemic to business require a transparency and an authenticity in our faith that aren't found in the rhythms of religion.

I've been hanging around the faith-and-work corner all my adult life. At times I tried to add catalytic thinking and enthusiasm. Other times I found myself researching and learning from the Scriptures, the thinkers of the past, and the leaders of the present. And sometimes I simply sat down on a bench and lingered, listened, and watched people of faith go to work every day. What a rich and challenging field trip it has been.

A Fresh Framework

As we shift to the next generation's leadership in every aspect of work, I want to keep the conversation going by offering a few thoughts and frameworks to help Boomers, Millennials, and Generations X and Z discover the power, reach, and intent of the gospel's going to work.

At the same time, I hope veterans of faith and work will be open to a fresh framework that could trigger a new level of leadership and impact. The gospel conversation can be either about you (the individual) or about the organization you work for. The gospel has both individual and organizational applications.

This Bible study is written not from the pulpit or the classroom to the workplace but from the workplace back to the church. In other words, my voice is that of a practitioner, not a preacher or professor. The approach is simple and practical, inviting you to agree or disagree with what I'm saying and to get actively involved in the learning process.

Passion

I love the weekends. But I gotta tell you, I love the weekdays just as much. Somewhere back in my younger life, the passion for taking the gospel to work grabbed me and has never released me. I hope this Bible study will share a bit of that passion with you.

WEEK 1
THE GOSPEL AND WORK

What makes up an average day for you? If you're like me, most of the best hours of most days are spent at work. You may be a young worker in the first ninety days of your job, a CEO considering your final three legacy years before retirement, or somewhere in between. No matter where you land on that continuum, if you're a follower of Jesus Christ, the question we all must answer is, What more can I do to integrate the gospel into my work?

Over the next six weeks we'll answer that question by using *The Gospel Goes to Work* grid. The gospel conversation can be either about you (the individual) or about the organization you work for. The gospel has both individual and organizational applications. Through personal reading and group discussion, you'll discover how this grid can provide a framework for taking the gospel to work.

BOTTOM LINE
The gospel affects all of life, including your work.

VIDEO SUMMARY

Use the statements below to follow along and take notes as you watch video session 1.

Scripture gives at least three catalytic metaphors, images that say, "This is what it looks like for faith or the gospel to show up anywhere." One is salt, one is light, and one is sweet perfume. How have you seen the gospel do its salt work, its light work, and its perfume work in a job setting? How do you see that taking place?

The power, reach, and intent of the gospel are much greater than we often realize.

No matter where we are on our journey of faith, every day that we go into work, we go into the largest mission field in the world. For me not to do that is missing a huge opportunity in the greatest mission field that exists. That's what gives me permission to show up at work and do what I do, which God has challenged me and called me to do, which may look very different from someone who has been called to sell everything and pack up and head out to a more traditionally described mission field.

CONNECT

1. When you were younger, what did you want to be when you grew up? What drew you to that profession?

2. Are you doing that job now? Why or why not?

EXPLORE

1. What first comes to mind when you hear the term *gospel?*

2. The Greek word for *gospel* means "good news." Read Romans 10:14-15. Notice that the apostle Paul celebrated Christians who understand their responsibility to proclaim the gospel with their words and their lives.

3. Evaluate yourself on understanding and sharing the gospel in your daily life. Share your thoughts about you and the gospel.

4. Why do you believe it's important for people of faith to take the gospel to work? What makes doing that hard and challenging?

5. How do you think it would affect your work life if you realized that work isn't a mundane, necessary part of your life but an opportunity to build the kingdom of God?

TRANSFORM

1. Consider the statement "Wherever you are, whatever you're doing, the gospel matters." What would it look like to bring the reach, power, and intent of the gospel to all dimensions of your life?

2. Would your coworkers say you have interest and energy in their world, or would they write you off as only self-serving? Why?

Close the group session with prayer. Ask God for grace to see opportunities to display the good news in your workplace and in every other aspect of your life.

DAY 1 SPIRITUAL WORK

Is your work spiritual work? This is an important question to answer. It's common in our day to think of spiritual work and secular work as being distinct and different. This way of thinking sees secular work as performed by laypeople and necessary for income. But after people have reached a more advanced level of spirituality, they must step aside from their secular work as plumbers, teachers, truck drivers, or salespersons and enter vocational ministry, which performs the real spiritual work. Those who think this way don't say that laypeople don't perform spiritual work. Laypeople do—but only intermittently when they pray, read Scripture, volunteer at church, or perform acts of service.

How often do you feel that you truly perform spiritual work?

The problem with this way of thinking is that the Bible doesn't agree with it. Notice what the apostle Paul said to the workers in first-century Colossae:

> *Whatever you do, do it from the heart, as something done for the Lord and not for people, knowing that you will receive the reward of an inheritance from the Lord. You serve the Lord Christ.*
>
> **COLOSSIANS 3:23-24**

All work is spiritual. Paul's point is that whom you work for is far more significant than what you do or where you work. The question "Is your work spiritual or secular?" is important. But Paul seems to tell us that the more important question is "Whom do you work for?"

A gospel-centered life is a way of thinking. Gospel-minded work starts with your mindset, your motivation, and your allegiance. We must begin to think of any vocation—from pastor to plumber, from missionary to brickmason, from chaplain to car salesperson— as spiritual work if it's ultimately done for Jesus.

What's one step you can take to set your mind on working for Jesus today?

DAY 2 THE CANVAS

Vincent Van Gogh, one of the world's greatest painters, was once quoted as saying, "I dream my painting and I paint my dream."[1] Whether or not he knew it, Van Gogh was borrowing a model from our Creator God.

Take a few minutes to read and meditate on God's creation account, found in Genesis 1. Which term describes your state of mind when you're reminded that God created everything that exists?

Awe	Excitement	Wonder	Joy
Confusion	Humility	Fear	Other:

Circle the five assignments that God gave to humankind in verse 28.

> *God blessed them, and God said to them,*
> *"Be fruitful, multiply, fill the earth, and subdue it.*
> *Rule the fish of the sea, the birds of the sky,*
> *and every creature that crawls on the earth."*
>
> **GENESIS 1:28**

From the very beginning, God involved humans in His good work. God's intention is for us to do His work in the world. The most important work in which He involves us is to spread the gospel of His Son, Jesus Christ. The gospel needs to be implemented in every area of our lives.

Underline an area of your life in which the gospel is bearing fruit.

Family	Work	Church	Hobbies	Friends	Other:

As you end today's study, circle the part of your life in which you'd most like to see the gospel have freer rein. Now pray that God will paint the entire canvas of your life with His good news.

DAY 3 GOSPEL GAPS

The world is God's canvas on which He's painting the powerful gospel story. Often He uses imperfect artists such as you and me to hold the brushes and even paint some of the strokes. But He wants the entire canvas covererd; that is, He wants all of life to reflect His goodness. God's desire is to paint His glory in every corner of the canvas of His creation.

Just turn on the news, and you'll be reminded that many areas of the canvas are desperate for God's goodness to be painted. We call these areas gospel gaps.

A gospel gap can be a spot in your life or your work that needs to be painted with God's goodness. Gospel gaps have their root in what theologians call the fall, a term that refers to the effects of sin on humankind and on God's good creation.

Read Genesis 3:14-19.

This passage describes the effects of sin on multiple domains of life: relationships, childbirth, the earth, and even work. When Adam and Eve sinned in the garden, it changed everything. The effects of sin splattered all over the entire canvas of God's good creation as evil set out to destroy God's goodness.

Circle the sin-affected gospel gaps in the world that burden you most.

Sex trafficking	Racism	Unemployment
Fatherlessness	Self-serving leaders	Unethical business
Abuse	Poverty	Other:

What's one gospel gap in your workplace, an area that sin tries to claim?

The remedy for any and all gospel gaps is an injection of the gospel in its full power, reach, and intent. As you conclude today's study, write a personal letter to God, asking Him to show you the gospel gaps in your life and work and expressing your desire for Him to repair them. Ask God to help you paint other gospel gaps in the world with His gospel. God can use any brush to color His canvas. Decide to let Him use you.

DAY 4 THE FOUR-ACT GOSPEL

Many Christians think of the drama of the gospel like a play with two acts: fall and redemption. In act 1 Adam and Eve's sin separated us from God, and humans would no longer be in perfect relationship with God. But in act 2 Jesus came, and now all who repent of their sin and believe in Him can be saved and made right with God. This narrative is beautiful and true. But it's not the whole story.

Read what God said to Satan in Genesis 3:15. Underline what He said the seed of the woman (Eve) will do to the enemy (Satan).

I will put hostility between you and the woman,

and between your offspring and her offspring.

He will strike your head,

and you will strike his heel.

GENESIS 3:15

God broke into the dark moment of Adam and Eve's failure to declare that all creation, broken by the fall, could be redeemed and renewed by the good news. This is the Four-Act Gospel.

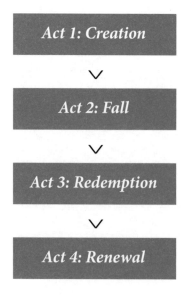

Act 1: Creation

∨

Act 2: Fall

∨

Act 3: Redemption

∨

Act 4: Renewal

If you realize that renewing a broken world is an aspect of what God is doing, this can make a big difference in the way you approach your work. Your work life can be a partnership with God in His work. Any worker, then, can apply the gospel in any workplace, doing any work that isn't inherently sinful.

The Four-Act Gospel reminds us that even our work plays a role in God's work to redeem and renew the world. The type of gospel we believe in makes a difference because it affects the way we think about our purpose in life. If we have a Four-Act Gospel, we'll be in the business of both helping individuals know Jesus and contributing to God's mission of renewing the world. It takes both to bring complete honor and glory to God. It takes both to paint His full story on the canvas of your life and work.

In what ways do you reflect a Four-Act Gospel in the way you do your work? Consider these specific expressions.

Creativity:

Failure:

Forgiveness:

Fresh starts:

DAY 5 THE FRAMEWORK

Today we'll introduce two concepts that are key to understanding how the gospel goes to work. We find them in Luke 3. This chapter tells the story of an untamed, rustic, no-holds-barred preacher named John. He was known for preaching a bold message of repentance and then baptizing the people who responded. One day a crowd had gathered near the Jordan River. As John preached, the crowds began to ask him how they should respond to his message. Check it out.

Read Luke 3:7-11. What was so bold about John's words?

Would you be interested in listening to a preacher like him? Why or why not?

John was preaching the gospel and calling the people to repentance. It was a message that applied to everyone in the crowd—young and old, male and female, rich and poor, rural and urban, and workers of all types. The gospel was a universal invitation, and generosity was the universal response. Reflecting the love of God for us through the way we treat others is what we call the Baseline.

BASELINE

The minimal gospel witness offered by any company
and its employees simply by the way they do their work,
regardless of location, personality, title, age, or background.

Now read Luke 3:12-14. The tax collectors and soldiers asked John how they needed to change in order to live the gospel message. What applications did John give them?

First notice what John didn't tell them. He didn't tell any of them to quit their jobs and join vocational ministry. He told them to go back and do their jobs in ways that honor the Lord. But he answered each profession—tax collectors and soldiers—according to the requirements of that profession. The application John gave is what we call the Blue Sky.

BLUE SKY
The boundless horizons of what could be when
a business or an employee personalizes an idea
or insight that contextualizes the gospel.

Based on what you read in Luke 3, what are some ways John might tell you to live out the gospel (Blue Sky) in your work or profession?

I hope the Baseline and the Blue Sky are beginning to give you a vision for addressing gospel fundamentals at work. Let's add one more layer to it.

The gospel conversation can be either about you (the individual) or the organization you work for. The gospel has both individual and organizational applications. When you merge the Baseline-Blue Sky pair with the individual-organizational pair, you get what we'll call *The Gospel Goes to Work* grid. With this grid you can begin to fill the empty spaces of life's canvas with gospel paint.

In the remainder of our study together, we'll explore each quadrant of this grid in great detail. But let's take a glance today.

INDIVIDUAL BASELINE
Employed followers of Jesus are accountable to represent Him by doing their work to the best of their ability.

INDIVIDUAL BLUE SKY
How workers tap into their imagination, wiring, and calling to harness the power, reach, and intent of the gospel through their work.

Think about a colleague at work. List some differences between you and him or her.

	YOU	COLLEAGUE
Background		
Education		
Family		
Personality		
Strengths		

Notice the differences between the two lists. Even two people working at the same kind of job at the same company can have drastically different personalities, interests, passions, and ambitions. Even if both of them are followers of Christ, they wouldn't express the gospel the same way. Because you're unique, I can't give you a list of what your Blue Sky actions are. But in week 3 I'll help you develop a vision for your Individual Blue Sky.

Think about it. If Christians lived out only the Individual Baseline quadrant and none of the other three, spiritual awakening would break out. But when Christians are embedded in an organization, some gospel-centered characteristics should naturally emerge. We call these the Organizational Baseline and the Organizational Blue Sky.

ORGANIZATIONAL BASELINE
Values and thresholds that any organization doing any kind of work should embody if it hopes to be a credible conduit for the gospel.

ORGANIZATIONAL BLUE SKY
Any organization can demonstrate God's renewal process in extraordinary ways in its specific industry by using imagination and inspiration to guide its operations to new outcomes.

Churches often hold celebration services to recognize and honor people whom God calls to the "sacred" work of vocational ministry. But in the same way God has called pastors and missionaries, He calls gospel-proclaiming men and women in every city and every community around the world. They occupy all industries and sectors. They're embedded in megaglobal companies. They own local bakeries or insurance agencies. They've launched their own social-media marketing firms. They coach junior-high basketball teams. When those men and women embrace and live out the realities of *The Gospel Goes to Work* grid, gospel movements can break out in workplaces everywhere.

1. Vincent Van Gogh, "Vincent Van Gogh Quotes," *Goodreads,* accessed February 1, 2017, https://www.goodreads.com/author/quotes/34583.Vincent_van_Gogh.

WEEK 2
INDIVIDUAL BASELINE

This week we'll consider a question you may have never thought about: What are the things all followers of Jesus, regardless of their skills and temperament, their work setting, and the kind of work they perform, can do to represent Jesus well? What about their employers or businesses? Are they operating in a way that glorifies God? You might wonder, *Is it even possible to come up with a list that will encompass the CEO and the factory-line worker, publicly owned corporations and mom-and-pop shops, manual laborers and office denizens?*

The answer is yes. We call that list the Baseline.

BOTTOM LINE
Every day at work is an opportunity
for gospel display.

VIDEO SUMMARY

Use the statements below to follow along and
take notes as you watch video session 2.

What are the things every follower of Jesus, regardless of their skills and temperament, their work setting, and the kind of work they perform, can do to represent Jesus well?

If every Christian did nothing else but get their skills up and deliver skill on a daily basis, at least there would be a little bit of an opportunity for a minigospel revival.

People of faith often have a different way they think about going to work. It's kind of like I work for two bosses. "You're my boss, Heather," "You're my boss, Charles," but I also have a heavenly boss. There's this notion that I'm on a divine assignment.

Calling looks like you care. You show up on time, doing what you said you would do.

CONNECT

1. Where's your favorite place to take a vacation from work? Why?

2. What are three things that make a vacation successful?

EXPLORE

Read 2 Timothy 1:8-12. The apostle Paul, while awaiting his death in prison, wrote to his friend Timothy to encourage him to faithfully continue the gospel work. Paul reminded him that God's calling in both of their lives meant that they were part of the bigger story God is writing.

Being called means being divinely assigned to do something for the Lord. Like Paul and Timothy, we're called to spread the good news of the gospel through our everyday lives, including our workplaces. That calling is for any worker, for any kind of work, and in any work setting.

Read Genesis 2:15. God created humankind in His image. Before sin entered the world, He placed Adam and Eve into the garden to work. This assignment was bigger than simply making money.

1. Have you most often looked at your occupation as an opportunity to reflect the image of God, create excellence, and live on mission or simply as a way to make money?

2. How would you describe the difference between being employed and called? How would you explain calling to someone with little or no influence in their organization?

3. Would your coworkers say you have interest and energy in their work, or would they write you off as only self-serving?

4. How would you define serving at work?

TRANSFORM

Close by praying. Thank God for His purpose in saving and calling you. Ask for courage and wisdom as you explore the ways you can live out His purposes in your everyday life.

DAY 1 BASELINE BENCHMARKS

Several years ago I was asked to speak at what was, at the time, a new men's ministry called Promise Keepers, an organization founded by former University of Colorado head football coach Bill McCartney. The particular event I was scheduled to participate in was at the Detroit Silverdome. The prospect was a little unnerving, considering nearly eighty thousand men would be listening to my every word. As I prepared to speak, I knew I wanted those men to know that through their work they could be part of God's plan. So I built my talk around this one question: What's the lowest common denominator for taking the gospel to work? As I prepared, the Lord led me to Psalm 78.

Psalm 78 beautifully describes God's purposes for His people. In verses 70-72 the psalmist painted a picture of God's sovereignty in choosing David to join Him in His mission for the world.

Read those verses below and circle key words.

He chose David his servant

and took him from the sheep pens;

he brought him from tending ewes

to be shepherd over his people Jacob—

over Israel, his inheritance.

He shepherded them with a pure heart

and guided them with his skillful hands.

PSALM 78:70-72

This passage offers four key benchmarks that make up the Individual Baseline. Recall the definition of *Individual Baseline* from week 1:

INDIVIDUAL BASELINE

Employed followers of Jesus are accountable to represent Him by doing their work to the best of their ability.

Anyone can use his or her calling, character, skills, and service to take the gospel to work.

The four Baseline benchmarks are listed below. Match the key words from Psalm 78 with the Baseline benchmarks to which you believe they correspond.

Calling	"skillful hands"
Character	"pure heart"
Skill	"his servant"
Service	"He chose David"

We'll study each of these benchmarks in depth over the rest of this week.

In which one of them would you say you are strongest?

In which one are you weakest?

Why did you answer the way you did?

Consider the benchmark you identified as your weakest. If it became a strength, what difference do you think it would make in you and in your work?

These four benchmarks are for men, women, executives, and hourly workers. When these benchmarks are implemented, they're like stones that, when mortared together, create a strong Individual Baseline for employees who want to go to work with the gospel. Tomorrow we'll define and examine the benchmark *calling*.

DAY 2 CALLING

One of the most common questions I hear from Christian college students is something similar to "How can I discover God's will for my life?" This is a great question because it has at its root the idea of calling. It likely assumes a few things. It assumes there's some-thing God wants me to do—a *why*. And it assumes that *why,* when I attach my life to it, is where I can find the most fulfillment and make the greatest Kingdom impact. Scripture tells us:

> *We know that all things work together for the good of those who love God, who are called according to his purpose.*
>
> **ROMANS 8:28**

Christians can be confident that God has a *why*—a Kingdom purpose—for our lives. The reality, however, is that most people live their entire work lives with no *why* other than making enough money to support their families. Regi Campbell said it this way: "The primary objective for most people's career is to eliminate the need for it."[1]

How motivated are you by a *why* to wake up each day and engage in your work?

1	2	3	4	5	6	7	8	9	10
Very little									It drives everything.

If you had a difficult time with that, you're … well, normal. Most people haven't thought about their callings that clearly. Often the only ones who have are in vocational ministry. But as we saw in week 1, God doesn't call only clergy. He calls all Christ followers. Second Corinthians 5:17-20 gives us a clear picture of what our *why* should be.

Read 2 Corinthians 5:17-20 in your Bible. Circle or highlight key words. What's the mission to which Paul said God has called us? The ministry of _____.

Renewal and reconciliation constitute the mission God is about in this world. He has invited us to use the way He has uniquely shaped each of us to join Him in that mission. Saddleback Church in California teaches its members to think through their callings by using the acronym SHAPE.[2]

Record your thoughts beside each of the following questions.

SPIRITUAL GIFTS: What gifts has God given you? (A ministry-gifts inventory is available at lifeway.com.)

HEART: What are you passionate about?

ABILITIES: What are you good at?

PERSONALITY: What's your personality type? (Christian personality assessments are available online.)

EXPERIENCE: What have been the major experiences, good or bad, that have shaped you?

To be called is to be released to be exactly who you're supposed to be and to do precisely what you're supposed to do for God. When you figure out your SHAPE, you'll be well on your way to being clear about your calling. What more compelling reason to get up when the alarm sounds each morning than to know that God has assigned your work and that He cares about its quality?

DAY 3 CHARACTER

Let's begin today's reading with a couple of questions.

What's one word you think someone at work would use to describe your character?

What word would you use?

What's your favorite form of art?

☐ Music
☐ Sculpting
☐ Painting
☐ Poetry
☐ Other:

In Bible days if an artist wanted to wear a groove into a metal plate, he would do so by repeatedly etching the same place with a sharp tool. After repeated strokes, an image would begin to take shape. The name for that tool in the Greek language is the word from which our word *character* is derived.

That word is used only once in the New Testament. Read that verse below.

> *The Son is the radiance of God's glory and the exact*
> *expression [character] of his nature, sustaining all things*
> *by his powerful word. After making purification for sins,*
> *he sat down at the right hand of the Majesty on high.*

HEBREWS 1:3

Think about the picture the writer of Hebrews was painting. The glory of God is exactly etched into the character of the Son. Just as an image of God is seen in the Son, when the character of Christ is etched into us, we present to the world a clear picture of the glory of God.

Think of someone you would say has great character. List three words that describe the person.

1.   2.   3.

Behavior and character are related, but they aren't the same thing. Behavior is what you do. Character, on the other hand, is the person your behavior has built. Behavior is just one action: "I behaved badly in that situation." Character is the sum of my behaviors—public and private—consistently arranged across the spectrum of my life. Any behavior—duplicated and reduplicated—forms a part of my character.

Every time you make a decision, you cut a groove. Every time you react to a crisis, you cut a groove. When you hold your tongue and practice self-control or when you let your tongue run loose and speak your mind, you're carving your character. When you say yes or no to a reckless temptation, you're signing your name. When you stand up to peer pressure, hold the line on truth, or return kindness for cruelty, you're cutting the pattern of your character. Here are a few examples of how this might look.

- The boss will treat his employees as human beings who have feelings, not as tools to accomplish his will.
- The marketing director who values honesty will practice truth in advertising and not exaggerate the company's services.
- The team leader who's striving for humility will resist the temptation to take credit for someone else's idea.
- The hourly worker will never cheat on the time he or she clocked in or out.

What habit can you begin today to express godly character at work?

No amount of business-ethics training has been able to establish consistent integrity in the workplace. But habits motivated by biblical faith and engraved into our character over time can turn the way we do business into a slight reflection of the flawless character of God.

DAY 4 SKILLS

In day 2 we talked about the importance of discovering your God-given SHAPE. Let's focus on the *A* in SHAPE, abilities or skills. Skills matter to God. God is a skillful God who performs all things with excellence. Because we were created in God's image, we have the capacity to appreciate and imitate God's excellence. That ability is clearly seen in Exodus 35. God was guiding His people to build the tabernacle, a place where they could commune with Him. Verses 30-35 name two men who possessed God-given skills.

Read Exodus 35:30-35. List the names of the men and the skills they possessed.

Name:

Skill:

Name:

Skill:

God created skills to be used for His mission of renewal in the world. When we use our skills, we reflect the excellence of God's image in which we've been created. For example, when a mechanic uses his skill to fix a problem that no one else can fix, when an entrepreneur creates a successful business from nothing, when a tenacious salesperson negotiates through almost insurmountable obstacles to close a deal, they reflect God's glory.

Booker T. Washington once observed, "Excellence is to do a common thing in an uncommon way."[3] What two skills can you execute with excellence that God can use to reflect His glory?

1.

2.

What two skills do you feel you need to develop more?

1.

2.

What do you value more—your job performance or your spiritual pursuit?

Often when faith goes up, skill goes down. For some strange and disturbing reason, it seems that when people become more passionate about their faith journey, they sometimes become less valuable at work. This is the opposite of the gospel going to work.

What can you do this week to reflect the glory of our excellent God while utilizing a skill He has given you?

As you end your study today, ask God to fill you with His Spirit, like Bezalel and Oholiab, and to give you opportunities this week to utilize your skills to glorify Him. This is how He has made you to work.

 # SERVICE

Today we'll focus on the fourth Individual Baseline benchmark, service. Let's begin by thinking about a simple definition of *serving*:

Serving is simply having the energy and focus for others that we find for ourselves.

Name someone you would classify as a great servant. What practical evidence have you noticed that would cause you to describe the person that way?

In Luke 10 Jesus told a story about an unlikely servant who went out of his way to give energy and focus to someone else.

Read Luke 10:30-37. What excuses might the two religious men have offered for not serving the man in need?

What common excuses do you offer for not serving?

Serving isn't a function of status, power, or station. Unless you're completely isolated from other people, you have the opportunity to model serving every day. Regardless of your occupation, title, and authority, if you work around people, you can model serving.

Let's consider what serving might look like in different work scenarios. Record what you might do to model serving in each of the four cases that follow.

A coworker is stressed with a deadline and needs help.

A colleague is being promoted.

You hear of an aspiration a coworker has.

During break time a group of coworkers are criticizing another coworker.

If any of these situations exist in your workplace, how will you serve this week to shine the light of the gospel?

Serving isn't easy. In fact, it's risky. People are messy. Serving is literally spending yourself on behalf of others. But remember, when you serve that way, you're modeling Jesus. No one embodied sacrificial service more than Him. You never know; by serving the way Jesus did, you may set off a chain reaction that ultimately changes the basic culture at your workplace.

We need to close this week's study with a word of caution. When it comes to the gospel going to work, the Individual Baseline must be the foundation. Without focusing on these four Baseline benchmarks, you'll actually hinder the gospel.

On the other hand, imagine what could happen if you devoted a year to practicing these benchmarks. What if you and your community of faith focused for one year on displaying godly character while serving the people around you? What if you showed evidence of God's calling on your life while you delivered God-given skill?

These four benchmarks alone—calling, character, skills, and service—could initiate a gospel movement reminiscent of great spiritual awakenings of past ages. Revival could break out in our churches, workplaces, and communities.

Do your part. Give God your calling, character, skills, and service and watch Him do a miracle with them.

1. Regi Campbell, *About My Father's Business: Taking Your Faith to Work* (Colorado Springs: Multnomah, 2005), 19.
2. Rick Warren. *The Purpose-Driven Life* (Grand Rapids, MI: Zondervan, 2002), 236.
3. Booker T. Washington, "Booker T. Washington Quotes," *BrainyQuote,* accessed February 1, 2017, https://www.brainyquote.com/quotes/authors/b/booker_t_washington.html.

WEEK 3
INDIVIDUAL
BLUE SKY

Before airmail, crop-dusting, the space shuttle, and drones, there were Orville and Wilbur Wright. The dreaming and innovation of these two brothers from Ohio brought about the first powered flight in history. Transportation would forever be changed because of what happened that day in Kitty Hawk, North Carolina. The Wright brothers were Blue Sky thinkers.

Last week we looked at the Individual Baseline, the starting place for all gospel expression in the workplace. This week we'll explore the Individual Blue Sky, the region of a person's work that taps into his or her wiring and calling to harness the power, reach, and intent of the gospel.

BOTTOM LINE
Work provides a platform for a particular expression of your redemptive story.

VIDEO SUMMARY

Use the statements below to follow along and
take notes as you watch video session 3.

Biblical principles teach you to think the way God thinks.

How many people out there have seen this modeled? It's a challenge to all of us to say, "I've known someone who lived, modeled, and verbalized their faith really well at work and actually made me change the way I thought about it."

I have trouble praying continuously, as 1 Thessalonians says, engaging God on a regular basis in my day-to-day work, even in the small things. So when I think about that spreadsheet I need to look at this afternoon, that doesn't feel like something I think I need to engage with gospel-minded thinking. That's a problem that I actually compartmentalize the small things.

Work is core throughout life. The gospel is literally core to our faith.

CONNECT

1. What did you enjoy as a child that you still enjoy today in your job?

2. What ideas stood out to you in last week's personal study? Why?

EXPLORE

Read 1 Corinthians 12:4-7. Paul pointed out that in a church there are different spiritual gifts, ways of serving, and activities to be involved in. The unifying factor is that the same God empowers every believer's gift or act of service in the body of Christ.

1. How does it feel to know that God has uniquely wired you to do what only you can do for the Kingdom? Do you feel that you're currently living out that wiring in ministry?

2. Why do you think a one-size-fits-all approach to applying the gospel at work doesn't work? Where and how does it break down?

3. Read Ephesians 2:10. Paul said we're God's workmanship, created for good works. What are some ways you can become more involved in the good works God has prepared for you to do?

4. In day 1 of this week's personal study we'll talk about David. At one point in his story he decided not to use Saul's armor. As effective as it was for Saul, it didn't fit David well enough to have the same effectiveness. How has God equipped you to be effective in taking the gospel to work?

5. Can you think of people who use their gifts and skills to do something exceptionally or uniquely well as an expression of the Individual Blue Sky at work? What have you observed about their effectiveness and success in their work?

TRANSFORM

What can you and your group do this week to help one another discover or use your unique wiring for gospel advancement at work? Close by committing these actions to God in prayer.

DAY 1 DAVID, THE BLUE SKY WARRIOR

No two jobs are identical. No two people are the same. Even if two workers do similar work, they aren't exact duplicates. This is why believers naturally personalize or customize our gospel applications based on who God made us to be, what kind of work we do, and the setting in which we're doing it.

> Have you ever been in a situation when you were tasked to do the same job as someone else? If so, recall the way you both did your work and the results. What was the same? What was different?

SAME   DIFFERENT

Often in situations like these, one or even both of the workers feel stress, tension, and a need to conform to the rhythms of the other. That's what David felt in his encounter with Saul in 1 Samuel 17. When we recall this story, we often think of David's defeating the giant warrior Goliath. Certainly he did. But there's more.

> Read 1 Samuel 17:38-39. After David volunteered to represent Israel and fight the mighty Philistine, what did Saul do?

☐ Required David to train with his generals
☐ Put his own armor on David
☐ Offered David a personal lesson in self-defense
☐ None of the above

> Identify three emotions David might have felt when, although he knew God wanted to use him for His glory in fighting Goliath, he wasn't even able to wear Saul's armor?

1.
2.
3.

When have you been required to "wear Saul's armor"? How did it make you feel? Describe your experience.

Read 1 Samuel 17:40. Instead of using Saul's gear to fight the giant, what did David use instead?

INDIVIDUAL BLUE SKY

How workers tap into their imagination, wiring,
and calling to harness the power, reach,
and intent of the gospel through their work.

Wisely, David took off the armor that was made for another warrior and selected some river stones for his sling—familiar weapons he had used to slay the bears and lions that attacked his father's sheep. Like David, we should reject approaches to living the gospel at work that might be fine for others but don't fit us. We must find a style that fits our own context, our own God-given wiring, and our own faith narrative in order to operate as effective Blue Sky warriors at work. Only when we minister to others and express the gospel from our unique set of abilities and gifts will we be able to find the most fulfillment and give God the most glory.

For the remainder of this week we'll consider four variables that differentiate you from other people and mold your unique expression of the gospel you show to the world around you.

DAY 2 GENERATION

Jane and Emma are physicians who work in the same clinic. Both are detail-oriented. Both care deeply about people. Both are Christians who want to represent the gospel faithfully. But Emma is 27, and Jane is 62. Are they going to represent the gospel in the same way?

When thinking through your own Individual Blue Sky, it's important to recognize that the generation in which you grew up will have a definite shaping effect on you.

What phrases have you heard your grandparents (or someone much older than you) say that you would never say?

Today's workforce is primarily made up of Boomers, Gen Xers, and Millennials. Following are a few characteristics of each.

BABY BOOMERS (BORN 1946–64): driven, workaholics, place high value on quality, initially skeptical of authority but becoming more traditional, desire to know, opinions matter, value personal gratification

GENERATION X (BORN 1965–80): educated, seek life balance, pragmatic, work to live, high job expectations, functional, fast-paced, flexible, self-sufficient, value diversity, willing to take on responsibility

MILLENNIALS (BORN 1981–2000): tech-savvy, highly tolerant, collaborative, place high value on fun, strong sense of entitlement, sociable—make workplace friends, place high value on making a difference in the world[1]

Each generation sees and engages with its world in drastically different ways. For example, Millennials will never know life without cell phones and laptop computers. When Boomers were in their teens and twenties, these inventions were only remotely possible.

It's important to understand that no generation is living out the gospel rightly or wrongly, just differently. The apostle Paul seemed to understand this. Notice what he said in his first letter to Timothy, his young protégé:

Don't let anyone despise your youth, but set an example for the
believers in speech, in conduct, in love, in faith, and in purity.

1 TIMOTHY 4:12

Summarize this verse in your own words.

Paul recognized the strengths of a different generation. The story of Abraham and Sarah also reminds us of the value different generations have in living out the gospel. When God wanted to build a nation through which the Messiah would eventually come, He called Abraham and Sarah, a couple in their nineties. Read Sarah's response:

Abraham and Sarah were old and getting on in years. Sarah
had passed the age of childbearing. So she laughed to herself:
"After I am worn out and my lord is old, will I have delight?"

GENESIS 18:11-12

With both of these Scriptures in mind, what do you think God would want to say to you today about the roles of different generations in representing the gospel at work?

List three general characteristics of your generation that will help you take the gospel to work.

1.

2.

3.

DAY 3 PERSONAL WIRING

Today we'll examine the variables that make you, you and what makes your work, your work. Let's discover why your personal wiring affects the way you live out your Individual Blue Sky in your workplace.

We're all made in God's image, but each one of us is beautifully crafted as a one-of-a-kind creation. This is what David was getting at in Psalm 139:13-14.

Read the verses below and underline the words that stand out to you.

> *It was you who created my inward parts;*
> *you knit me together in my mother's womb.*
> *I will praise you*
> *because I have been remarkably and wondrously made.*
> *Your works are wondrous.*
>
> **PSALM 139:13-14**

Take a few minutes to pray this psalm. Writing your prayers is good for the soul. Record your prayer in the space below.

Rick Warren, the pastor of Saddleback Church in Southern California and the author of *The Purpose-Driven Life,* articulates individual uniqueness with the acrostic SHAPE:

S   Spiritual gifts

H   Heart

A   Abilities

P   Personality

E   Experience[2]

We'll look at spiritual gifts, heart, and abilities today and explore personality and experience tomorrow.

SPIRITUAL GIFTS. God has given all of us spiritual gifts. They have a direct bearing on the way each of us reflects the gospel at work. For example, someone with the gift of mercy might want to join a community-outreach program, while someone with the gift of teaching might give compelling presentations that honor God by their excellence.

> Read the lists of spiritual gifts in Romans 12:6-8 and 1 Corinthians 12:8-10. Record each gift Paul mentioned.

> Circle the spiritual gift(s) you believe you have.

HEART. This component of your wiring is about what makes your heart come alive— what are you're passionate about. Kirk is an insurance agent who loves football. So he supports his local high-school football program by volunteering as a coach. It's important to pay attention to your unique passions and allow God to use them to bring about His purposes where you work.

> What makes your heart come alive? How could you use those passions at work?

ABILITIES. What are you good at? Everyone has a unique set of abilities that God can utilize as each person takes the gospel to work. For instance, Bill is a metalworker. He has made items like custom gates and ornamental curtain rods for years. He uses his abilities to offer excellent work at affordable prices to his clients. He has also volunteered his time and materials to build custom pulpits for churches.

> What unique abilities do you possess that could show up in your Individual Blue Sky? How could God use them to take the gospel to your workplace?

DAY 4 PERSONALITY AND EXPERIENCES

Yesterday we began looking at your unique personal wiring by exploring the acrostic SHAPE.

Recall the elements you studied yesterday and record them here.

S

H

A

P   Personality

E   Experience

What did you learn about your wiring in yesterday's personal study?

What did you learn about God?

PERSONALITY. What's your personality type? God gave all of us different personalities. Some of us are energized by people. Others are energized by being alone. Some are visionaries. Others pay great attention to details. Some are task-oriented. Still others are deeply concerned about the feelings of other people. Understanding your temperament is critical to recognizing how you can express the gospel in ways that are uniquely you.

Mark the point where your personality falls on each scale.

People-oriented	Task-oriented
Extrovert	Introvert
Big-picture	Detail

Now use that information to describe your personality in a couple of sentences.

EXPERIENCE. Consider all the experiences you've had, good or bad. These help outline your context, the filter through which you experience life. Though you may have the same temperament, abilities, and even spiritual gifts as someone else, your unique life experiences will give you opportunities to take the gospel to work in an individual way. For example, Jean and John are both pharmacists who work at the same pharmacy. They're even said to resemble each other. But there's one striking difference: Jean is a cancer survivor. She allows that experience to fuel ways she expresses the gospel at work as she counsels, supports, and serves patients who come in to fill cancer prescriptions.

What are three life-shaping experiences you've had?

1.

2.

3.

How can you use those experiences for the sake of the gospel?

Identify one experience that you may not consider life-shaping but that God has used.

When you discover your SHAPE, you'll be able to more completely recognize ways God has personally wired you to bring Him glory in your workplace through your Individual Blue Sky.

DAY 5 CONTEXT

The gospel can go to work with any worker in any work setting. But the way that happens can look beautifully diverse.

List the first five occupations that come to your mind.

1.

2.

3.

4.

5.

You likely thought of a few more than five. Even the Bible mentions dozens of jobs. Gideon was a farmer. Dorcas was a seamstress. Luke, a doctor. Daniel, a government official. The point is, because there are thousands of types of businesses and jobs, there are also literally thousands of ways the gospel could be taken to work.

Go back to the five jobs you listed. Think of ways someone working in each one of them could take the gospel to work. List one idea beside each job.

Taking the gospel isn't limited to certain types of jobs. Brian Dijkema writes:

> We get excited about those who open local coffee shops or become journalists or start a nonprofit or (fill in the blank). But what do our "faith and work" books have to say to people who work on the line at a Ford assembly plant, or to medical assistants who take care of the elderly? Will landscapers and receptionists see themselves in the "work" we're talking about?[3]

Blue-collar and white-collar jobs both offer many opportunities to take the gospel to work. The jobs may look different because of the settings and circumstances, but those settings and circumstances create unique ways to live and share your faith. Recall Bill, the metal-worker we spoke of in day 3. By making beautiful designs and donating his time to local churches, he strives to bring glory to God.

Effectiveness for the gospel is similar to brand impressions on social media. If you want to get your brand across on social media, you need lots of tweets and posts that reach many followers. Similarly, our culture needs many gospel impressions if it's going to close the gospel gaps. The advancement of the Kingdom requires a broad diversity of individuals who are expressing the true gospel through their Individual Blue Sky. Only when you're making your own unique contribution to spreading the gospel will the gospel color the complete canvas of your work life. And you'll be able to give God all the glory.

> End this week's study by thinking about representing the gospel in your context. Use the space below to identify ways you can tap into your Individual Blue Sky in order to harness the power, reach, and intent of the gospel.

1. Generational Differences Chart, accessed February 2, 2017, http://www.wmfc.org/uploads/GenerationalDifferencesChart.pdf.
2. Rick Warren, *The Purpose-Driven Life* (Grand Rapids, MI: Zondervan, 2002), 236.
3. Brian Dijkema, "The Work of Our Hands," *Cardus*, March 1, 2015, http://www.cardus.ca/comment/article/4411/the-work-of-our-hands/.

WEEK 4
ORGANIZATIONAL BASELINE

Just as there's a baseline for individuals, there's an organizational baseline for treating people and creation in ways that honor God's values. There are some irreducible minimums that apply to any and every organization that wants to do good. If you want to be a part of an organization that lives out the gospel, you must help it live up to the baseline. And if you're a Christian, you should want to be part of an organization that, at minimum, tolerates gospel goodness.

Any organization that wants to allow the gospel to flow through its culture is anchored to certain common baseline practices. This week we'll explore five of them.

BOTTOM LINE
Leadership that's rooted in the gospel
brings a redemptive edge to any culture.

VIDEO SUMMARY

Use the statements below to follow along and
take notes as you watch video session 4.

The gospel can show up in the organization, and over time the organization can do different and be different.

How can you not be a roadblock so that the gospel can just flow through what you do for your employer?

There are a lot of people in the nonprofit world who want to help and want to do good. One key concern is for them and the nonprofits is how to approach social-justice issues from a gospel framework.

The gospel is not always loud and overt. It doesn't always have to hang on the corridor walls, sing in the lobby music, or scream from the website. It's more embedded than that.

CONNECT

1. What was the biggest idea you recall from last week's personal study? Why?
2. Look at the plan you made for your Individual Blue Sky in day 5 last week. What's something specific you want to put into practice?

Imagine what could happen if the power of Christ followers could be harnessed in an organization to maximize the gospel's effectiveness. The results would be incredible. That's the possibility we'll explore this week as we focus on the Organizational Baseline.

EXPLORE

1. Do you believe there are universal best practices any organization can use to reflect the gospel? Why or why not?
2. If there was disagreement in your discussion, it likely centered on the idea of Christian versus non-Christian companies. Do you believe it's possible for even non-Christian companies to express the gospel? If so, how?
3. Describe the universal minimum for any organization to be gospel-minded.
4. How have you seen your product or your firm's interaction with communities work redemptively?
5. Share examples of companies that do a great job of revealing God and His ways to people. What's the gap between these companies and yours? What can you do about it?
6. Read Matthew 20:20-28. James and John's mother approached Jesus and asked Him if her sons could sit in places of honor in the Kingdom. How do you think Jesus' response relates to an Organizational Baseline at work?

This week we'll explore the Organizational Baseline, which is built on five foundation stones. When a company's employees recognize the value of turning from inward to outward, they can begin to influence their work culture. Gospel-centered workers must learn the value of serving others.

TRANSFORM

Finish this week's group by reading aloud John 15:5. Discuss ways you can help one another abide in Christ this week. Pray for grace for group members to abide in Him so that you can bear much fruit and so that He will be glorified.

DAY 1 FOUNDATION 1: MULTIPLE BOTTOM LINES

This week we'll examine the Organizational Baseline, the set of threshold values and actions that a business needs to have in place in order to represent the gospel. Five foundation stones support the Organization Baseline. The first is multiple bottom lines.

A single numerical figure at the bottom of a balance sheet, regardless of its size, can't be the only metric by which an organization measures success. Our whole world is quickly migrating toward an expectation that all efforts return something beyond a single bottom line. For some time people have talked about the double bottom line—aiming for profits and something else. In 1994 John Elkington coined the phrase "triple bottom line." His three bottom lines were people, planet, and profit.[1] In 2006 Andrew Savitz continued the dialogue by publishing a book called *The Triple Bottom Line,* which emphasized the social, environmental, and financial performance metrics for success.[2]

> Think about the company you work for. Does it recognize multiple bottom lines or only one? List them here.

Savitz is on the right track, but he's missing the piece that should fuel it all: the gospel. He doesn't separate the spiritual good from the social good. Companies that are fueled by the gospel and work toward multiple bottom lines have what could be called a redemptive edge.

Although a number of possible bottom lines could affect the Organizational Baseline, we can consider them in terms of four categories:

1. **PROFITABILITY.** The obvious one. Are you making money?
2. **ENVIRONMENT.** Is your work replenishing the earth? Is it sustainable?
3. **SOCIAL GOOD.** Are you providing jobs, opportunities, and social welfare for others?
4. **SPIRITUAL RETURN.** Is faith being strengthened? Is the gospel being displayed as part of this work?

If you're an organizational leader, multiple-bottom-line thinking protects you from everything you don't want to become, and it's your power to bring about the change you dream of.

How can your organization's leaders develop multiple bottom lines in the following categories?

Profitability:

Environment:

Social good:

Spiritual return:

Read the definition of *Organizational Baseline.* How could these bottom lines shape your organization's Baseline to reflect the gospel in your workplace?

ORGANIZATIONAL BASELINE
Values and thresholds that any organization
doing any kind of work should embody if it
hopes to be a credible conduit for the gospel.

Multiple-bottom-line thinking can help define your business's Organizational Baseline because it puts your company's convictions to work. At the same time, it can be good for business. Happier employees, shareholders, and customers usually produce a higher-achieving and more stable company.

DAY 2 FOUNDATION 2: GRACE AND TRUTH

Amazing grace! how sweet the sound
That saved a wretch like me!
I once was lost but now am found,
Was blind, but now I see.[3]

The words of this old hymn may take you back to the small country church where you grew up. Or maybe your grandmother played it on the piano as she sang great hymns of the faith. For followers of Jesus, this beautiful declaration of amazing grace should instill wonder as we gaze on the cross, remember the price Jesus paid for our sins, and consider the redemptive story He invites us into.

When we feel the weight of grace, we'll be people of grace. And we want to be people of grace.

The second foundation stone of the Organizational Baseline is grace and truth. The first question we need to ask today, as we think about the gospel going to work, is, How can grace live in a fierce business culture? We often think of grace as something that could work only in the world of nonprofits but never in corporate America or in a mom-and-pop business.

In what (legal) industry do you think it would be most difficult for grace to thrive? Why?

Grace can thrive in any business anywhere, but it doesn't come naturally. Yet when organizations intentionally develop rhythms of grace in the DNA of the business, they contribute to a happy, productive staff and create a long-term reputation for trustworthiness in the marketplace.

Healthy organizations are also infused with a culture of truth. Read these words of Jesus:

Jesus told him, "I am the way, the truth, and the life.
No one comes to the Father except through me."

JOHN 14:6

If we're followers of Jesus, the Truth, our lives must be characterized by truth. When we embody truth, the organization we're a part of is rooted in truth.

How could hearing the truth in your business setting create opportunities to learn and apply the grace of the gospel in that setting?

When an organization creates a culture of grace and truth, those characteristics become foundation stones that the Organizational Baseline is built on.

DAY 3 FOUNDATION 3: STEWARDSHIP

So far this week we've talked about two of the five foundation stones that the Organizational Baseline is built on.

Recall the foundation stones we've studied and record them here.

Foundation stone 1:

Foundation stone 2:

The third foundation stone that supports a strong Organizational Baseline is stewardship. Every organization must determine how to get its best return on investment from all the assets that are working on behalf of the company. This is what stewardship is. Peter Block defines *stewardship* this way: "To hold something in trust for another." He also writes that stewardship is "the willingness to be accountable for the well-being of the larger organization by operating in service, rather than in control, of those around us."[4]

How would you define *stewardship* in your own words?

One of the clearest pictures of stewardship in the Bible is presented in Genesis 39.

Read Genesis 39 in your Bible. Recall the details here.

Who was the steward?

What was he in charge of stewarding?

Whom did he serve as a steward?

Joseph stewarded resources well—well enough, in fact, that he was promoted to a high post in Egypt. Eventually, God used him to deliver his own nation, Israel, from famine.

What resources have you been put in charge of stewarding for your organization?

How well do you think an observer would rate you as a steward in your job?

1	2	3	4	5	6	7	8	9	10
Terribly									Very well

When people of faith lead organizations, they should consider their jobs to be stewarding the resources of their organizations for God. But even when leaders of an organization aren't believers, they can think of themselves as stewards on behalf of humanity's common good or the next generation.

Stewardship involves financial resources, but it also involves human resources. There are typically three ways companies handle human resources:

1. **COERCION:** forcing someone to do what you want through intimidation and threats
2. **INCENTIVE:** offering a commission, a raise, or perks if the employee's sales, productivity, or performance increases
3. **INSPIRATION:** showing employees that they're part of something big and exciting, then enlisting their support

Have you ever been part of an organization that tried to coerce enthusiasm? How successful was that effort?

Using the terms above and applicable Bible verses you can recall, describe the human-resources strategy you believe would lead employees to flourish in your organization.

Stewardship is a Baseline value that motivates an employee to figure out what the corporation's dreams and aspirations are and to help the management realize them. Stewardship is an underutilized driver of behavior that can be harnessed to benefit an entire organizational culture.

DAY 4 FOUNDATION 4: HUMBLE COLLABORATION

Companies that reflect a gospel Baseline recognize the value of working together and not thinking too highly of self. Humble collaboration, the fourth foundation stone of the Organizational Baseline, refers to people getting a task done together rather than in isolated silos.

It might surprise you to discover that collaboration isn't simply a human innovation. It has its roots in the Trinity. Consider this verses:

> *Just as the body is one and has many parts, and all the parts of that body, though many, are one body—so also is Christ.*
>
> **1 CORINTHIANS 12:12**

What do you notice in this verse that points to the idea of collaboration?

The context of this statement is Paul's call for unity in the body of Christ. But the practical outworking of collaboration could certainly apply to work. The apostle Paul reminded the church in Corinth of the uniqueness each member brings to the congregation. So it is at work. When a company values collaboration, even if it isn't a Christian organization, that company models a biblical principle.

Let's take that a step further. Look back at the last phrase in 1 Corinthians 12:12. Paul was saying that working in uniqueness and unity, or collaboration done well, is a picture of Christ. This is a reference to the Trinity. Within the Trinity are God the Father, God the Son, and God the Holy Spirit. Each Person of the Trinity is distinct in role, yet all three work together in perfect harmony to accomplish the mission of God.

What strikes you most about this principle of humble collaboration? Record your thoughts.

Few companies collaborate as well as Pixar. Ed Catmull, the chief executive officer, described its collaborative process this way: "People at all levels support one another. Everyone is fully invested in helping everyone else turn out the best work. They really do feel that it's all for one and one for all."[5]

This is only one example of collaboration. Collaboration can be a freeway system for the gospel to travel. On the other hand, noncollaboration can be a disappointing dead end or a stifling roadblock.

Which of the following might be reasons for rejecting collaboration? Circle all that apply.

Insecurity	Competition	Ambition	Greed	Personality type
Holiness	Selfishness	Focus	Drive	Strategy
Productivity	Other:			

Have you ever been to a symphony? The way each artist plays together under the guidance of the conductor is a beautiful picture of the way collaboration could work in an organization. One psychology professor said it this way:

All great inventions emerge from a long sequence of small sparks; the first idea isn't all that good, but thanks to collaboration it later sparks another idea, or it's reinterpreted in an unexpected way. Collaboration brings small sparks together to generate breakthrough innovation.[6]

Imagine if a saxophone player or, even worse, an entire section of instrumentalists began to play in a different key or in a different rhythm. The result would be a dissonant mess. So it is with many organizations. Often the pursuit of competitive advantage has replaced working with others to accomplish a greater good. Eventually, an unhealthy independence can destroy a company's collaborative culture and fracture its Organizational Baseline.

If siloing and a lack of collaboration are common in your organization, what's one action step you can take this week to move the dial toward collaboration?

If your company already does well with collaboration, what step can you take to maintain and improve it?

DAY 5 FOUNDATION 5: LOVE

How does the organization you work for treat people? Your answer will reflect your company's Organizational Baseline. Every organization has a reputation, both inside and outside, in regard to human resources. Companies may treat their employees like material assets, useful for little more than helping them meet their financial goals, or like real people with families, struggles, debts, and illnesses.

Think about the way your company leads, communicates with, and motivates employees. Rate where you believe your company is on the scale.

1	2	3	4	5	6	7	8	9	10
Simply assets									Real people

In *The Hungry Spirit* Charles Handy prophetically proclaimed:

> ## Businesses, then, and indeed all institutions, are communities not properties, and their inhabitants are to be more properly thought of as citizens rather than employees or human resources.[7]

A kernel of the gospel is embedded in his approach to people. Think about it.

What's the difference between thinking of people as citizens and treating them simply as employees?

Someone once asked Jesus which was the most important commandment. He responded, "Love the Lord your God with all your heart, with all your soul, and with all your mind" (Matt. 22:37). Then He added a second. Do you remember it?

Read Matthew 22:39 and record it.

The Greek language has four words that all translate into our word *love*. In English, if we desire to express our affinity for pizza, a friend, or a spouse, we use the word *love*. In Greek a different word would be used for each type of affection. The word used in these verses comes from the root *agape,* which isn't an emotional love but a selfless action, regardless of feelings or circumstances.

Organizations that wish to implement the gospel Baseline must build it on the foundation of love. Even if you aren't the chief executive officer of your company, you can still help create a grassroots-grown culture of love in your workplace. Joel Manby argues in *Love Works* that you should "lead with love."[8]

Businesses demonstrate love by the way they motivate people, pay people, communicate with people, and tell the truth. They treat workers with kindness, fairness, dignity, justice, and compassion. Some companies set aside an emergency fund to help employees who are going through hardship. Others pay for their employees' children to go to college. Still others collect money at Christmas to help workers who don't have enough money to buy presents. Companies that want to build a strong Organizational Baseline are intentional about treating people decently and redemptively.

> Ask God to show you one action you can take during the next week to take *agape* love to work. Record your thoughts here.

These days our navigation software often has us "drop a pin" to state, in effect, "Here's where I am or where I want to go." It's a way to guide our movement toward a goal or clarify our starting point. Let's agree to drop a pin on the Organizational Baseline to remind ourselves that love is the starting point for gospel impact.

1. "Triple Bottom Line," *The Economist,* November 17, 2009, http://www.economist.com/node/14301663.
2. Andrew W. Savitz with Karl Weber, *The Triple Bottom Line,* rev. and updated (San Francisco: Jossey-Bass, 2014).
3. John Newton, "Amazing Grace! How Sweet the Sound," *Baptist Hymnal* (Nashville: LifeWay Worship, 2008), 104.
4. Peter Block, *Stewardship: Choosing Service over Self-Interest,* 2nd ed. (San Francisco: Berrett-Koehler, 2013), xxiv.
5. Ed Catmull, "How Pixar Fosters Collective Creativity," *Harvard Business Review,* September 2008, https://hbr.org/2008/09/how-pixar-fosters-collective-creativity.
6. Keith Sawyer, *Group Genius: The Creative Power of Collaboration* (New York: Basic Books, 2007), 102.
7. Charles Handy, *The Hungry Spirit: New Thinking for a New World* (London: Arrow, 1998), 179.
8. Joel Manby, *Love Works: Seven Timeless Principles for Effective Leaders* (Grand Rapids, MI: Zondervan, 2012).

ORGANIZATIONAL BLUE SKY

This week we will talk about the fourth and final quadrant of the framework, the Organizational Blue Sky. Chuck Colson once said, "Christians are called to redeem entire cultures, not just individuals."[1] Because all of our organizations are diverse, their expressions of the gospel are diverse as well. Imagine the impact on the cultures of organizations all over the world when each of them begins to color the canvas that God has given them with the beauty of the gospel. This is why this quadrant of the Baseline-Blue Sky framework possesses such great potential for gospel impact. Yet it's the most underdeveloped.

BOTTOM LINE
A community of people who share the bond of faith can eliminate the gospel gaps in any industry and institutionally push back darkness.

INDIVIDUAL BLUE SKY

ORGANIZATIONAL BLUE SKY

INDIVIDUAL BASELINE

ORGANIZATIONAL BASELINE

VIDEO SUMMARY

Use the statements below to follow along and
take notes as you watch video session 5.

A gospel gap is a pattern of behavior that needs supernatural reversal. Look at your job, your team, and the work you're doing and identify where gospel values aren't prevailing. Then pray and act to inject gospel goodness into those gaps.

You've got to provide an environment where people are willing to get on the edge. You've got to be passionate about taking care of your customers. You've got to remove fear, and that goes with leadership. Once we defined that culture for everybody and gave people permission to behave that way, it took a while, but there was a collective sigh of relief that said, "Well, OK; I can just be me."

In the nonprofit sectors, nonprofits are notorious for wanting to be all things, provide the entire supply chain. They don't want to partner. They don't want to collaborate, because when you collaborate, you're giving up some power or leverage, so we become something that does it all. A lot of competition happens; a lot of duplication of services happens.

If churches want to do mentoring programs, instead of doing your own thing, partner with another organization that's doing a similar thing. While it might not be under the faith banner, Christ is still present. God uses even nonbelievers to do His work.

CONNECT

If you had the power to change one problem in the world today, what would it be?

This week we'll look at the fourth quadrant in the gospel matrix, the Organizational Blue Sky. If Christians in organizations all around the globe focused on maximizing the potential of the gospel in and through their organizations, entire cultures would be transformed, and many of the world's problems would be eradicated.

EXPLORE

1. Take a few minutes to discuss last week's personal study. What are the five foundation stones of the Organizational Baseline? Which one resonates most with you?

2. How could a gospel focus solve a problem in your company or department?

3. Chuck Colson once said, "Christians are called to redeem entire cultures, not just individuals." Do you agree? Is that possible in every industry? Why?

TRANSFORM

Read Acts 8:1-4. After the stoning of Stephen, many believers dispersed throughout Judea and Samaria. Saul (also called Paul, who later had a transformative encounter with the Lord) not only approved of the execution of Stephen but also made a daily practice of dragging Christians out of their homes to be imprisoned and often killed. His efforts didn't stop the gospel from spreading. We may not be under persecution in the same way, but we'll face opposition when we seek to glorify God and embed the gospel in our workplaces.

What's one way a group of believers at work can hold up one another when opposition comes?

1. Chuck Colson, as quoted in Abraham Kuyper, *Wisdom and Wonder: Common Grace in Science and Art* (Grand Rapids, MI: Christian's Library, 2011), 15.

DAY 1 BLUE SKY REGIONS

Gospel impressions through both Individual Baseline and Blue Sky (weeks 2–3) are very important. So is devotion to gospel values at the Organizational Baseline level (week 4). Yet quadrant 4, the Organizational Blue Sky, has the greatest potential for gospel impact because organizations have great multiplied power to bring about either poor consequences or good ones. Let's recall the definition of *Organizational Blue Sky:*

ORGANIZATIONAL BLUE SKY

Any organization can demonstrate God's renewal process in extraordinary ways in its specific industry by using imagination and inspiration to guide its operations to new outcomes.

Think about the organization you work for. Would you consider it an organization that uses its resources to multiply the impact of the gospel? Why or why not?

How does your organization go beyond the Organizational Baseline to demonstrate God's renewal process in extraordinary ways?

Because organizations are diverse, their expressions of the gospel will be diverse as well. A one-size-fits-all answer won't work when you want to emphasize the gospel message in a particular work setting. You've got to figure out what the gospel might look like when it expresses itself through your particular organization at a particular time. Let's explore that concept.

List three different companies.

1.

2.

3.

Each one of the companies you listed is unique. In regard to the gospel, every company you thought of and every company in the world falls into one of three macroregions in the Blue Sky. We'll introduce them today, then examine them throughout this week.

REGION 1: THE GOSPEL FLIES UNDER THE RADAR

Organizations in region 1 aren't likely run by Christian leaders. They don't offer goods or services that are visibly connected to the gospel. Faith doesn't influence the way this organization is run in public. However, at some level one or more team members in the company seek to share the light of the gospel. Therefore, the gospel stealthily infiltrates pockets of the organization while flying under the radar.

REGION 2: FAITH GUIDES THE ORGANIZATION

Is faith a public informer and guide for the language, culture, and operations of your organization? If so, it's a region 2 organization. In this model the organization has been imprinted by the gospel, and it's evident to those who come in contact with the company on any front. The most familiar example of a region 2 organization is Chick-fil-A, founded by Truett Cathy. Though the company doesn't offer Christian products and services, the organization is built in such a way that the gospel is manifested in every corner of the business. The gospel influence shows up in the business's commitment to customer service and in practices like Christian music playing in its restaurants.

REGION 3: THE COMPANY IS FAITH-DRIVEN

Region 3 organizations offer products and services that are overtly faith-oriented or faith-driven. In region 3 the gospel presumably permeates the inner working of the organization as well as the image it presents to the public. Its very reason for being is to promote the Christian faith. Examples are companies like LifeWay Christian Resources, Catalyst, and local churches.

What clarity has God given you today about how you can make the gospel more obvious in your organization? Record your thoughts.

DAY 2 REGION 1

Yesterday we introduced the three Organizational Blue Sky regions in which all companies can be categorized in their relationship to the gospel. Today let's explore what it looks like to work in a region 1 company, where the gospel must fly under the radar. The reality is, most of us are likely in this region because the majority of publicly owned companies are in this region.

Do you think people of faith work in every Fortune 500 company?

With few exceptions Christians are embedded in every Fortune 500 company, simply flying under the radar. One or more people may aspire to help the organization operate in a way that distinctly honors God. They want their company to be a conduit of the gospel, even though a Christian witness must be done outside the spotlight. There are millions of these individuals all over the world.

Jonathan lives in Tennessee, where he works for Nissan. His job is to drive the newly assembled Nissan automobiles from the end of the assembly line to the lot where they're parked to await distribution. His mission as a deeply committed follower of Jesus is to color the gospel on the Nissan canvas. He works closely with Jim, a non-Christian who spends most weekends getting drunk, and with Alice, who is Hindu.

What's one challenge you think Jonathan may face in his mission?

Men and women in region 1 companies, without question, will face unique challenges, so let's look at some of those challenges for employees who are operating in region 1.

CHALLENGES FOR REGION 1

WAIT FOR GOD'S TIMING. There are region 1 companies from California to Connecticut and beyond, where Christians dispense the gospel under the radar in their little corners of the companies. But because we want the gospel to flourish, we assume it has to be above the radar. However, if we push too hard or move too fast, this attempt never ends well. It's best to wait until God has prepared a heart to be receptive to the gospel.

One biblical example of running ahead of God's timing is found in Genesis 16. Impatient Abram and Sarai, seeking to fulfill God's promise of a child their own, assumed God would use another woman who wasn't already past childbearing age as Sarai was.

Read Genesis 16 in your Bible. What conflicts were brought about because of Abram and Sarai's impatience?

Gospel-centered workers must be able to discern the right circumstances and the appropriate times to introduce the gospel, perhaps when a personal need or crisis arises in a coworker's life or when an unexpected opportunity occurs at work. If you don't wait for the right time and place, the credibility of your witness could suffer. If you position yourself as someone who is pushy, abrasive, or "always right," people won't listen when you share the gospel. Instead, they'll shield themselves from you.

Have you ever experienced or observed circumstances or opportunities like these? Describe how the gospel was represented at work.

STRIVE FOR EXCELLENCE. Make sure you and your department or team are performing at a high level. Poor performance doesn't honor the Lord. It will also dilute the gospel paint you want to apply to your work canvas and will render your witness useless. Gospel workers don't necessarily have to be the top salesperson or employee of the month. But our jobs must display that we're people of excellence who work for a greater purpose: reflecting the image of our excellent God and bringing glory to Him.

What's one step you can take this week to do your work in a more excellent way?

How can waiting for God's timing and striving for excellence allow you to affect the Organizational Blue Sky where you work?

DAY 3 REGION 2

Yesterday we discussed region 1, where the gospel must fly under the radar. Today we'll turn our attention to region 2—companies where it's OK to be public about the gospel and where it's easier to find Organizational Blue Sky opportunities.

> **Record the name of a large city near you.**

> **How many region 2 companies do you know of in this city?**

We often don't know about these companies until they become regional or national, such as Chick-fil-A or Hobby Lobby. But there are thousands of them. Consider the large number of mom-and-pop companies in the city you named.

Denny owns a small construction company named Kingdom Construction. His intention to paint the beauty of the gospel everywhere he goes is evident even in the name he gave his company.

Lance is a physician who sees his medical practice as a ministry. He prays with his patients and cares for families with the understanding that he's only a practitioner who ultimately trusts in the Great Physician.

Scott owns a computer repair company called Integrity Computer Concepts. His understanding of computers and his heart for families give him the unique expertise to speak to church groups and parent-teacher organizations about Internet safety for kids.

> **List three region 2 organizations you're aware of. What strikes you most about them?**

CHALLENGES FOR REGION 2

TAKE INITIATIVE. Imagine there are two insurance companies on the same street. ABC Insurance is a region 1 company. The owner, Jim, has been to church only once in his life. When his brother died in a car crash, he attended the funeral. But he blames God for his brother's death and has come to resent the church as well. In his own words, he "never wants to step foot in that place again."

XYZ Insurance is a region 2 company. Sandy, the owner, is more than a casual church member. She sings in the choir, teaches children's Sunday School, and reads her Bible during the week.

> As Thanksgiving approaches, the local homeless shelter looks for donations of turkeys to feed the homeless. Which insurance company would you expect to be the first company to volunteer? Which would be more generous?

Lead your team, coworkers, or business to take initiative to display the gospel in outrageous ways. Lead the way in providing volunteers for the local high-school concession stand, serving at a crisis-pregnancy center, donating blood, or collecting food for the poor.

> Read Matthew 20:26-28. How do these verses apply to your company?

SERVE OTHERS. John owns a small region 2 company of between seventy-five and one hundred employees that services one of America's largest retailers. To say his company has done well would be an understatement; he became a millionaire in a relatively short period of time. Though John could have started frequenting finer restaurants, he didn't want to boast or suggest that he was entitled to material blessings because he was a Christian. Instead, he saw his habit of eating lunch at the same restaurant on the same day as a way to build gospel-centered relationships with the servers and patrons. When a waitress told him that she was going to be baptized, she thanked John for being a consistent picture of Jesus, always kind, honest, and respectful to everyone. John understood that even believers can be tempted to serve self instead of knowing and serving others.

> How does the company you work for serve others?

> What's one way you can help your company use service to be more public about the gospel?

DAY 4 REGION 3

Region 3 companies are businesses whose very reason for being is to promote the gospel. These are Christian businesses and ministries. As with regions 1 and 2, region 3 organizations acknowledge a few challenges in exploring their Blue Sky. Let's examine them.

CHALLENGES FOR REGION 3

FOCUS ON INFLUENCING CULTURE. Region 3 companies sometimes start comparing their effectiveness in expressing the gospel and influencing the world with the effectiveness of other Christian ministries. When that happens, the focus is shifted away from spreading the gospel and making disciples of Jesus—the very reasons these companies exist.

Jesus cautioned Christians to let their good works be seen for a singular purpose: to inspire others to glorify the Father.

Read Matthew 5:14-16. Summarize Jesus' caution.

When region 3 companies focus on something other than Christ, the light of the gospel is hidden and therefore never lights the world as it should. Organizations in region 3 must remember that God has given them their own unique Blue Sky opportunity, a mission that's distinct from the opportunities He has given the other region 3 organization down the street. Ministries and Christian businesses must stay focused on producing the fruit God has designed them to produce rather than inspecting the fruit of other organizations.

When have you observed comparisons being made between region 3 organizations?

What might these comparisons communicate to a lost world that's watching?

MAINTAIN AN OUTWARD FOCUS. The gravitational pull of every region 3 organization is inward. Leaders of these organizations must remain intensely focused on fighting against that gravity so that they can focus outward on the needs of the world.

The pastor of a growing, century-old church near Nashville, Tennessee, felt compelled to lead the congregation to avoid turning inward. Like a lot of churches of that size, it had the resources to provide recreational opportunities for the church members. In a physical display of its desire to stay focused outward, the congregation decided to donate the basketball goals from their family-life center to a local school in the community.

Instead of holding leagues that church members would participate in, the church canceled its congregational leagues and instead began training coaches from the church to go into the community's recreation leagues. The church's athletic program guided people from the church to the various community teams, a move that positively served the community and made the church's outreach more effective.

You might not work at a region 3 organization, but you're probably a part of one—a local church, where Blue Sky opportunities are wide open.

What has your region 3 organization or your local church done to maintain an outward focus?

How can maintaining an outward focus enable a region 3 company to influence culture?

DAY 5 PULLING IT ALL TOGETHER

This week we've looked at three regions of gospel influence in the business world:

REGION 1: The gospel must operate under the radar.

REGION 2: There is freedom to share the gospel.

REGION 3: The company is a Christian ministry.

Ask any person of faith who works in any one of the regions we've talked about this week, and you'll learn something about how the gospel can transform the culture of a business.

What region is your organization in?

How could a gospel focus correct a problem in your department, company, or industry?

Now consider this. Is it possible that a believer could be called to work in a region 1 company for the rest of his or her life? We shouldn't think of the three regions as tiers of value in propagating the gospel. Advancing in spiritual maturity doesn't mean we must leave one region and seek employment in the more spiritual next region.

Why does God call believers to work in region 1 companies, in which they have fewer opportunities to share their faith?

It's important to remember that each Blue Sky region holds equal significance and value. No one region of the Blue Sky is better than another in terms of propagating the gospel. Conduits for the gospel are found in organizations from all three regions.

EMBRACE THE BASELINES

It's important to remember that no matter what region a business is in, if the gospel is going to be believable, we must make sure believers are embracing both the Individual and Organizational Baselines and are actively working to represent Christ on those levels. If Insurance Agent Sandy and Dr. Lance aren't embracing the Baselines and caring for the people they're committed to serve, it makes no difference how many turkeys they give away or patients they pray with. They simply won't be taken seriously when they start to share the gospel. As we saw in Matthew 5:14-16 yesterday, if we aren't embracing the Baselines, we're blocking the light Jesus wants us to shine.

As you come to the end of this week's study, ask God to give you a vision for how you can help your organization live in the gospel Blue Sky. Some leaders in companies can pray publicly with people during a crisis. Others can't. Some organizations can visibly reflect the owners' and leaders' personal faith journey. Others can't. No matter where you are on the organizational chart or which region your company is in, you can still take the gospel to work in your particular setting.

What role can you play in the days ahead to maximize the Organizational Blue Sky potential in your workplace?

What are three action steps you'll take to fulfill that role effectively?

1.

2.

3.

Organizations are powerful. God can use them to paint His truth across the big canvas of our lives and His world. That's why the Organizational Blue Sky has the greatest potential for making an enduring impact with the gospel. Organizations have great multiplied power to bring about gospel movements. How big is your vision for what God could accomplish through your organization to renew the world?

WEEK 6
TAKE THE GOSPEL
TO WORK

Throughout this Bible study you've examined different building blocks of strategies for taking the gospel to work. As you come to the close of this study, you'll be challenged to use your spiritual imagination to develop a *Gospel Goes to Work* action plan.

Americans who have jobs spend an average of forty-seven hours a week at work. Sleep is the only close runner-up.[1] Imagine what could happen if you made a plan to leverage those forty-seven hours every week for the sake of the gospel and for the advancement of the kingdom of God.

BOTTOM LINE
One person living out the gospel can change
the world through his or her work.

VIDEO SUMMARY

Use the statements below to follow along and
take notes as you watch video session 6.

Much of the gospel that's shared seems to be evangelizing and moralizing. While those
certainly aren't bad, the challenge is to somehow get beyond just those two tasks, not
to redefine the gospel but to stretch the power, the intent, and the reach of the gospel
to other horizons—to our work and everywhere else. The gospel can and must make
a difference in things we do or can't do, whether in our negotiations, our actions,
or our conversations in and around work.

God has a bigger work here at our company. How can I be a part of that?

Some of the biggest issues, hurdles, or challenges to taking the gospel to work:

- Fear, because a gospel vision isn't shared by the company leadership
  or the owner
- Ourselves, because we're broken and sinful, and we make mistakes
- Busyness, because our world isn't slowing down, and sometimes
  the pace of the work gets in the way of my sharing the gospel

You make mistakes, but over time you grow.

CONNECT

1. Look back over everything you've studied for the past five weeks. What have you learned about God? About yourself?

2. How has thinking about the four quadrants of *The Gospel Goes to Work* grid challenged your thinking about the gospel?

EXPLORE

Read Matthew 5:14-16. Imagine the context in which Jesus shared these words. At that time, when you were outside at night, there were no streetlights or billboards to provide light. In that culture, when it was dark, it was really dark.

1. What are three results that could come about when believers let their light shine at work?

2. Identify a gospel gap in your community (for example, methamphetamine manufacturing, homelessness, hunger, divorce, gangs, or crime). How could your organization minister to that gospel gap?

3. If all Christians in every business in your community decided to let their light shine, what could be the effect on gospel gaps?

4. What's the first gospel gap you would like to eliminate in your community? How can you play a part, through your work, in filling that gap?

TRANSFORM

Close your final group session by encouraging one another to take the gospel to work. Then pray by name for each member of your group and each organization represented.

---

1. Lydia Saad, "The 'Forty-Hour' Workweek Is Actually Longer—by Seven Hours," *Gallup*, August 29, 2014, http://www.gallup.com/poll/175286/hour-workweek-actually-longer-seven-hours.aspx.

DAY 1 SALT, LIGHT, AND SWEET PERFUME

As we've seen throughout this Bible study, God calls Christians to join Him in His mission of redemption. The gospel goes to work when followers of Jesus live with a catalytic vision of being change agents in every domain of their lives—especially at work.

The Bible offers three pictures of what it looks like to take the gospel to work: salt, light, and sweet perfume. Let's explore them.

SALT

Read Matthew 5:13. Why do you think Jesus used salt to describe His followers? Record your thoughts.

Salt is a distinctive compound that's used primarily for two purposes: preservation and flavor. Jesus said Christians who have been sanctified by the gospel should preserve and flavor their culture with the gospel.

Think back. How is your life different because of the salt of the gospel?

Think ahead. How will the gospel penetrate, permeate, and alter your work?

LIGHT

Read Matthew 5:14-16. How do you see the light of the gospel shining through your employer or fellow employees?

What types of good works could you or your organization target to glorify God?

SWEET PERFUME

Read 2 Corinthians 2:15-16. How can the aroma of Christ represent both life and death?

How can Christians be the fragrance of Christ at work?

Salt, light, and perfume are change agents. They can transform what they come in contact with in positive ways. A dash of salt, a ray of light, and a dab of perfume give us examples of what happens when Christians touch culture the right way.

Consider a basketball coach who is taking the gospel to the high school where he works. His goal is not only to win basketball games but also to do it in a way that teaches his players how to be men. The coach teaches his players to be salt, light, and sweet perfume by giving them simple life examples. For instance, he tells them if they're walking down the street and see a piece of trash, they should pick it up. No matter where they find themselves, they should make that place better. Instead of blaming someone else in a given situation, they should address the needs they encounter.

What difference do you believe the coach's idea of responding to needs could achieve?

What conditions do you see at work that you could make better?

As you end today's study, ask yourself, *What's God saying to me about representing the gospel at work?* Record your thoughts.

DAY 2 SAVED TO SERVE

William Wilberforce has long been viewed as a hero, a Kingdom change agent, and a statesman-saint who was committed to bringing the redemptive edge to all his life touched after his encounter with God's amazing grace. As a reformer, philanthropist, and long-term member of the British Parliament, Wilberforce was a perfect illustration of someone who understood and lived out the Four-Act Gospel.

Nothing that's happening in our current culture and in our businesses today is more challenging than what Wilberforce faced. For example, during his time in leadership, Britain was the mind and muscle behind human trafficking (the slave trade) worldwide. It was so entrenched that even people of faith had learned to turn a blind eye to it. But William Wilberforce and his associates refused to simply let this gospel gap grow any wider.

As Wilberforce thought about his conversion and his calling, he asked himself a pivotal question: Why had God saved him? Chuck Colson summarizes Wilberforce's conclusion this way: "If Christianity was true and meaningful, it must not only save but serve."[1] Yes, the gospel had saved his soul. But the gospel wasn't only for him to "consume." It was to serve all humanity in redemption and renewal. For Wilberforce, serving meant finding the gospel gaps in his particular industry (politics and government) and addressing them with the gospel. He spent his entire adult life doing that.

> Would you say you're a person who has only consumed the gospel without serving others with it? Why or why not?

A more recent hero who unleashed the power, reach, and intent of the gospel into culture was the late Bob Briner, the author of *Roaring Lambs*. I remember being with Bob in his home one Saturday morning discussing his passion to fill the gospel gaps in the entertainment and media industries. Bob deeply believed:

If a religion is really vital, meaningful, relevant, and important, it will make a difference not only in the lives of individuals but also in society itself.[2]

List specific ways that you can convey in your work that the gospel is—

vital:

meaningful:

relevant:

important:

Both Wilberforce and Briner strongly believed what Chuck Colson later said: "Christians are called to redeem entire cultures, not just individuals."[3] I firmly believe there are gospel and work heroes in every city and every community around the world. We just don't happen to know them all. They're embedded in megaglobal companies. They own small local bakeries or insurance agencies. They've launched their own social-media marketing firms, and they coach sports teams. They occupy all industries and sectors.

Every community has men and women who are putting the gospel to work. Those who work next to them and live in community with them know them as catalytic vessels of the salt, light, and sweet perfume of the gospel. However, there's a secret. They don't argue about the different sizes, shapes, and colors in which the gospel is packaged; rather, they focus on getting the salt out of the shaker, the light powered on, and the perfume out of the bottle.

When that happens, the gospel goes to work. And when the gospel goes to work, mini-Kingdom movements begin. It's impossible for the salt, light, and perfume to do their work without resulting in transformation.

The gospel's power, reach, and intent are truly revolutionary, even for veterans of the faith. Put the gospel to work and start a minimovement.

Think about what could happen if the Christians in your workplace realized that they were saved to serve. How would your work environment look different than it currently does? Record your thoughts.

DAY 3 MODERN-DAY RESET

Let's begin today by reading a verse you've likely heard if you've been around church very much. In Luke 10:2 Jesus was preparing to send out the seventy-two on mission. Before He did, he told them something that shaped the way they and we should view our role in sharing the gospel.

> Read Luke 10:2 in your Bible and summarize it here.

Jesus often used the illustration of harvesting grain as an example of advancing the Kingdom. Let's view this verse through the lens of *The Gospel Goes to Work* ideology. Three key elements in this verse will lead us to a modern-day reset.

THE FIELD

When the color of grain changes from green to sun-bleached white, everyone can see that the crop is ready to be harvested. If the grain isn't harvested, it will go to waste. In your organization there are times and seasons—opportunities for Christians to apply the power, reach, and intent of the gospel to the harvest of souls. These opportunities may arise when your coworkers experience physical, emotional, or financial needs or times of great success, either planned or unexpected. In your workplace the harvest is ready in the field and plentiful. As workers in the field, we must be prepared when the harvest is ready.

> What events have you seen in coworkers' lives that might indicate a readiness to receive the gospel?

> What can believers do to be prepared when the harvest is ready in their workplace?

THE WORKERS

You may have thought of the workers in this account as representing people today who are willing to share an outline of the plan of salvation or even move to another country to live as a missionary. They're certainly included. But that understanding is too narrow. The application Jesus made here was community-wide. Jesus was saying every available person—every Christian in every job—is needed to work in the harvest.

When workers go into the field, they leave gospel footprints with every step. And if they're intent on working in the harvest, they'll come away with an abundance of grain, saved from waste and ruin, and destined to be of service in the kingdom of God.

Let's think about this modern-day reset of Luke 10:2 in practical terms. Record a couple of sentences describing what the result could be if believers in your workplace waded into the harvest-ready field.

When Christian workers catch a vision for the potential harvest and express the gospel at work, the gospel will pervade their organizations more powerfully. When the gospel is known, felt, and experienced, good things will happen. Imagine what would happen if all Christians applied themselves to working in the harvest. If every believer in every company in every workplace prayed and watched for the harvest, change would occur. When faithful workers enter the field, gospel footprints will be seen. Families will stabilize, churches will grow, and culture will change.

Close today's reading by asking God to unleash the gospel in your workplace in the same way Jesus sent out the seventy-two in His day. Record your prayer.

DAY 4 PLAN THE WORK AND WORK THE PLAN

Today we'll formalize a framework that will serve as your plan of action for taking the gospel to work. The gospel is intended to penetrate, permeate, and alter the way you consider and do your work. Because your work covers so much of the canvas of your life, applying it can be revolutionary, even for veterans of the faith. You may want to review some of the notes you've made in previous weeks as you complete the following components of your action plan to take the gospel to work.

WHAT IS

First let's review and evaluate your current situation.

Rate how well you believe you're doing on the four Individual Baselines.

Carry out calling.	1	2	3	4	5	6	7	8	9	10
Display character.	1	2	3	4	5	6	7	8	9	10
Utilize skill.	1	2	3	4	5	6	7	8	9	10
Model service.	1	2	3	4	5	6	7	8	9	10

Describe your SHAPE.

Spiritual gifts:
Heart:
Abilities:
Personality:
Experience:

Rate your company on how well it's doing on the four foundations of the Organizational Baseline. Evaluate only your work team or department if that would be more helpful.

Multiple bottom lines	1	2	3	4	5	6	7	8	9	10
Grace and truth	1	2	3	4	5	6	7	8	9	10
Stewardship	1	2	3	4	5	6	7	8	9	10
Humble collaboration	1	2	3	4	5	6	7	8	9	10
Love	1	2	3	4	5	6	7	8	9	10

Which region is your company in?

WHAT COULD BE

Describe ways you can take the gospel to work in the four quadrants of the Baseline and Blue Sky framework.

Individual Baseline:

Individual Blue Sky:

Organizational Baseline:

Organizational Blue Sky:

Your final step is to create a personal vision statement for taking the gospel to your workplace. Here's an example:

As I live the Baselines, express my unique
SHAPE, and work with the heart of a servant,
five years from now the negatives in my
company's culture will be completely replaced
by a culture of celebration and joy.

Now tailor this vision to your specific context.

What's your long-term vision for taking the gospel to work (think five to ten years)?

DAY 5 SPIRITUAL IMAGINATION

The Baseline and Blue Sky formula works for people of faith and for our organizations. This framework helps us move beyond conventional thinking tied to the lower-left quadrant, the Individual Baseline. It anchors us to nonnegotiables but also opens the door to dreams about gospel impact.

The gospel story transforms the hearts of people. With it one single transformed heart can inject salt, light, and sweet perfume that can alter an entire company over time. Kingdom movement happens when the gospel goes to work.

In all likelihood you've never heard of Edward Kimball, a Sunday School teacher who was deeply committed to living out the Four-Act Gospel of creation, fall, redemption, and renewal. In his class of rambunctious boys, one of them, Dwight, never seemed to pay much attention to his teaching. So Kimball went to the shoe store where the boy worked. While Dwight was stocking shoes, Kimball explained the gospel to him. Right there in his workplace, that teenager trusted Jesus. Dwight L. Moody would go on to take the gospel to the corners of the globe as one of the greatest preachers of his day.

The story doesn't stop there. Through Moody's efforts a man named J. Wilbur Chapman was reached and changed by the gospel and became a preacher. One day a young professional baseball player named Billy Sunday heard him preaching the gospel and believed. Sunday became a traveling evangelist, and as a result of his proclamation of the gospel, a man named Mordecai Ham came to faith in Jesus. Ham also became a traveling evangelist. While he was preaching in North Carolina, a lanky teenager called Billy Frank responded to the gospel. Billy Frank would go on to take the gospel to literally more people than anyone before him. Billy Frank's full name was William Franklin "Billy" Graham.[4]

What strikes you most about this story?

What does this story have to do with the gospel going to work?

In this story we see the power, reach, and intent of the gospel. It's interesting that this chain of events began with someone who wasn't a preacher, a missionary, or a theologian. Edward Kimball was simply a man who developed a passion to embrace the Baselines and to strive for the Blue Sky. He simply lived in a way that allowed the gospel to be painted in every corner of the canvas of his life.

Dwight L. Moody's conversion in, of all places, a shoe store reminds us that gospel movements that reach millions of people can begin with just one person. When Edward Kimball took the gospel to Dwight L. Moody's workplace, Moody's life and the lives of millions of people would never be the same. Moody would later say, "The world has yet to see what God can do with a man fully surrendered to Him. By God's grace I'll be that man!"[5]

Will you be that man or that woman? Close this study by summarizing and personalizing Moody's statement in a prayer of commitment to take the gospel to work. Record your prayer here.

Imagine what God will do when employees in all industries and on all rungs of the corporate ladder embrace the principles we've studied and apply them to our specific work environments. Imagine what will happen when the gospel goes to work!

I used to ask God to help me. Then I asked if I might help Him. I ended up by asking Him to do His work through me.[6]
HUDSON TAYLOR

1. Chuck Colson, preface to *William Wilberforce, A Practical View of Christianity* (Peabody, MA: Hendrickson, 1996), xii.
2. Bob Briner, *Roaring Lambs: A Gentle Plan to Radically Change Your World* (Grand Rapids, MI: Zondervan, 1993), 56.
3. Chuck Colson, as quoted in Abraham Kuyper, *Wisdom and Wonder: Common Grace in Science and Art* (Grand Rapids, MI: Christian's Library, 2011), 15.
4. Travis Agnew, "The Chain of Events Leading to Billy Graham's Conversion," *TravisAgnew.org*, July 22, 2013, http://www.travisagnew.org/2013/07/22/the-chain-of-events-for-billy-grahams-conversion/.
5. Dwight L. Moody, as quoted in Paul Chappell, "What God Can Do with a Surrendered Life," *DailyintheWord.org*, July 16, 2012, http://www.dailyintheword.org/rooted/what-god-can-do-with-a-surrendered-life.
6. Hudson Taylor, "Twenty-Seven Hudson Taylor Quotes," *Christian Quotes*, accessed February 6, 2017.

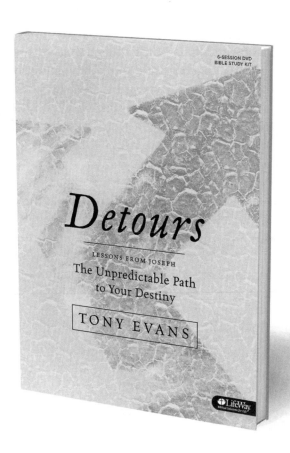

Has your career ever taken a DETOUR?

This message from Tony Evans is too good to keep to yourself. Fortunately, it's easy to share with your small group (or just a group of friends). The *Detours* Bible study includes step-by-step plans for six group sessions, leader tips, a promotional video you can use to invite people, 25- to 30-minute teaching videos featuring author Tony Evans, and more.

Bible Study Book Item 006104401
Bible Study Kit Item 006104403
Hardcover Book ISBN 978-1-4336-8659-7

LifeWay.com/Detours

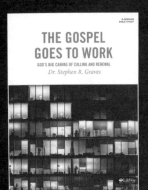

WHERE TO GO FROM HERE

We hope you enjoyed *The Gospel Goes to Work*. Now that you've completed this study, here are a few possible directions you can go for your next one.

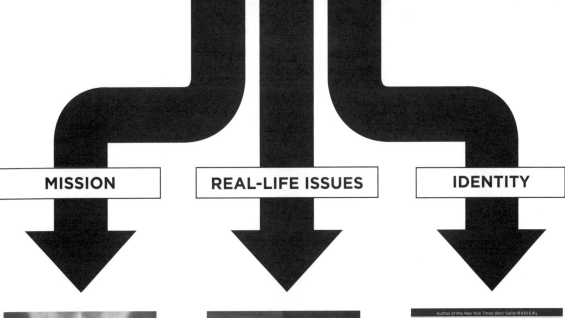

MISSION

REAL-LIFE ISSUES

IDENTITY

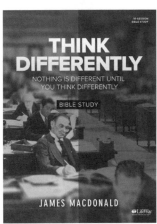

Learn a simple and relational approach to witnessing that underscores dependence on God's power for the result. (4 sessions)

Learn to renew your mind in Christ as you identify and overcome the mental, familial, and even self-created strongholds that enslave you. (10 sessions)

Challenge the traditions of cultural Christianity, and examine the meaning of Jesus' simple command: "Follow Me." (6 sessions)